THE COMET

BY

BETSY A. RILEY

BLUE DRAGON PRESS

MARYLAND

Published by Blue Dragon Press
visit our website at **www.bluedragonpress.com**

ISBN-13: 978-0615475783 (Blue Dragon Press)
ISBN-10: 0615475787

THE COMET

In her dreams
she was a comet.

The comet shone
in the dark skies of deep space,
sparkling, burning,
as she danced across
the heavens.

From a distance
she seemed to be
made of fire,
leaving a flaming trail.
But she had been
formed of ice.

A blazing cold streak,
she was a brittle beauty
traveling the universe . . . alone.

And she was lonely.

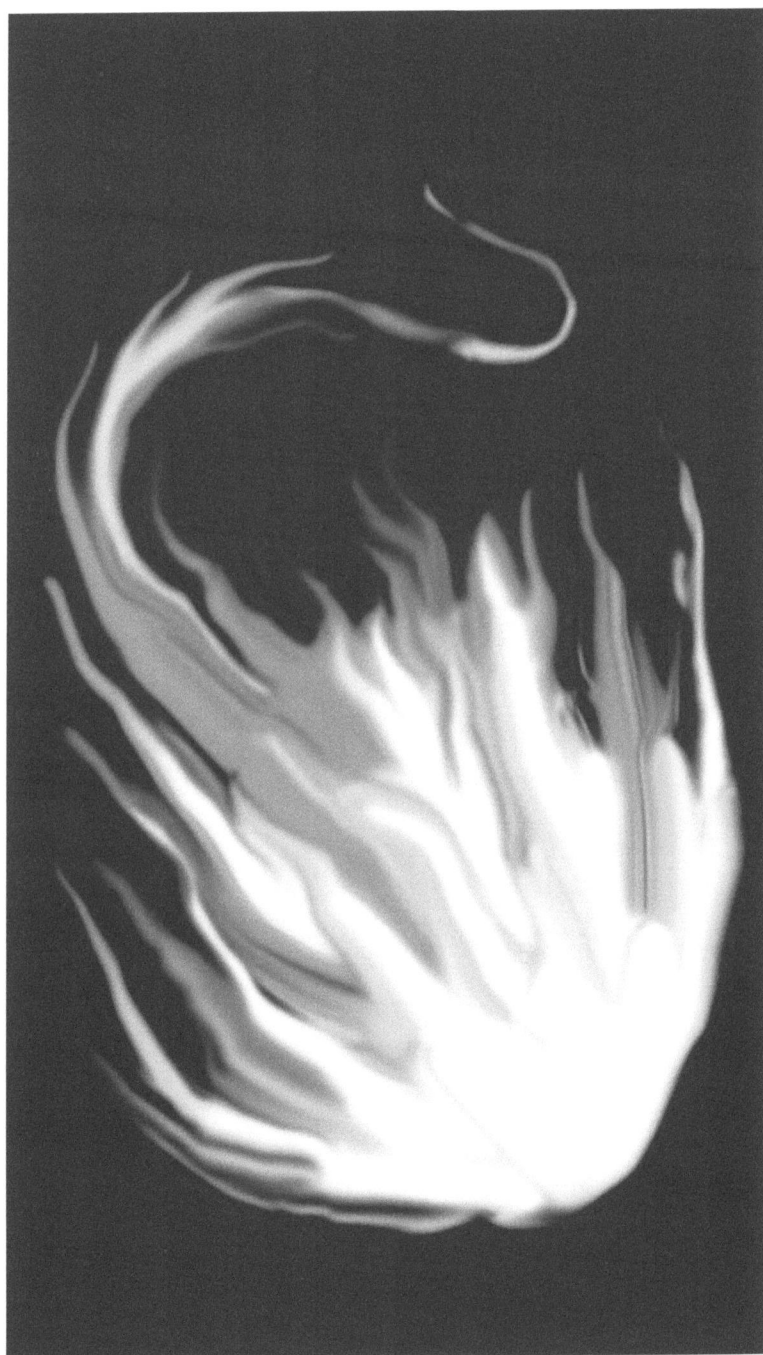

Spying points of light far away,
the comet raced towards them.

She called a greeting,
but there was no answer.
The stars were too distant, and
did not even sense her approach.

The comet danced
within a nebula,
enjoying its beautiful colors.

She called a greeting,
but the nebula did not answer.

Its very being was spread
far and wide,
too thinly to notice
such a concentrated mass as she.

So the comet traveled on, alone.

A moon caught the comet's notice.
It was a frozen orb,
circling a warm planet.

"Oh moon, talk to me, be my friend,"
the comet called, "I will tell you stories of
my travels and you can tell me
your dreams -- then perhaps we can
travel and dream together."

But the moon refused. It was enthralled
by the planet and dwelt in constant
attention to it, never turning away.

"I can't go with you, I must continue
my dance with the planet -- it needs me,
I light up its night skies and move
its tides -- it is my life and my love."

So this is love? the comet wondered,
Perhaps I should find love
so I won't be so lonely.

And the comet traveled on.

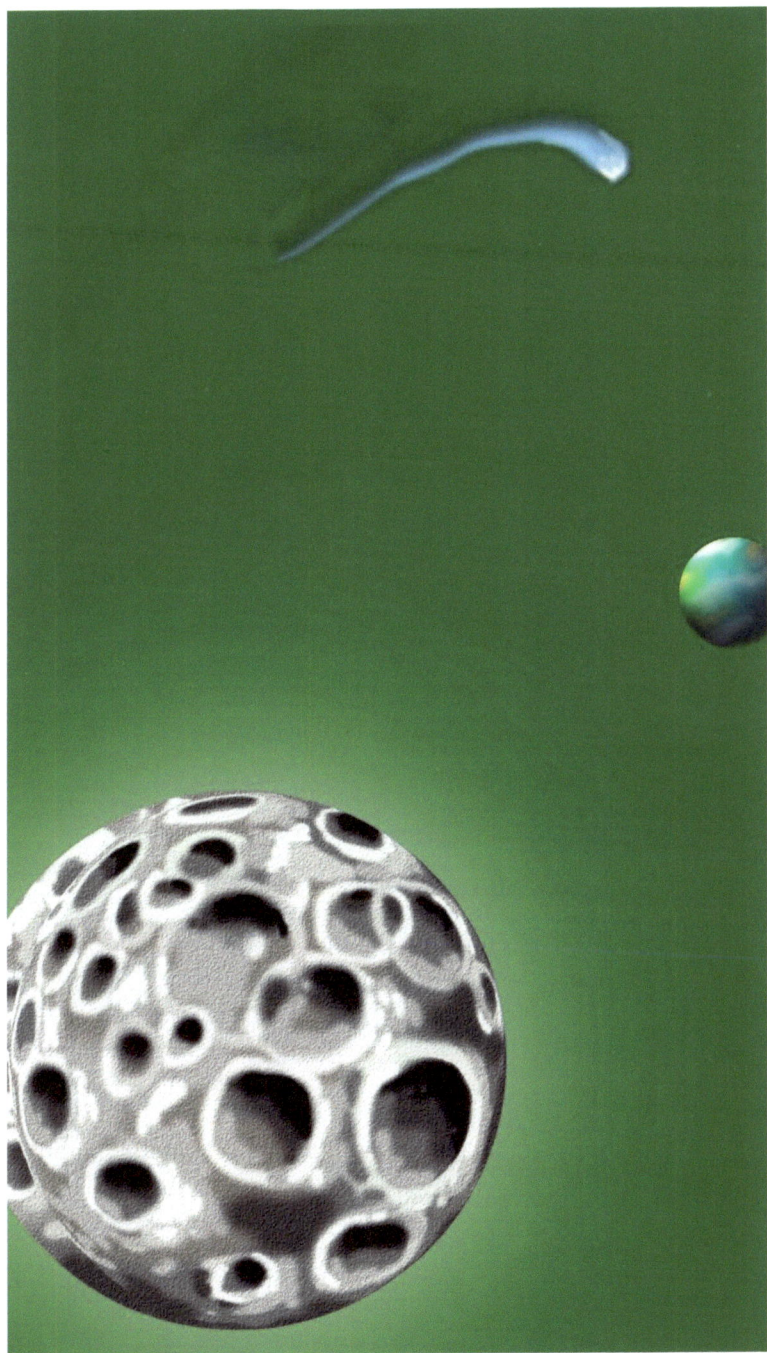

The comet traveled past
many planets, but they all
had their own moons.

She passed a band of asteroids,
barren blocks of rock
that seemed to once have been
planets or moons.

Now they were lifeless shells.

Seeing them,
the comet wondered
if such a lifeless existence
was to be her destiny.

But the distant points of light
still sparked her imagination.

So the comet traveled on.

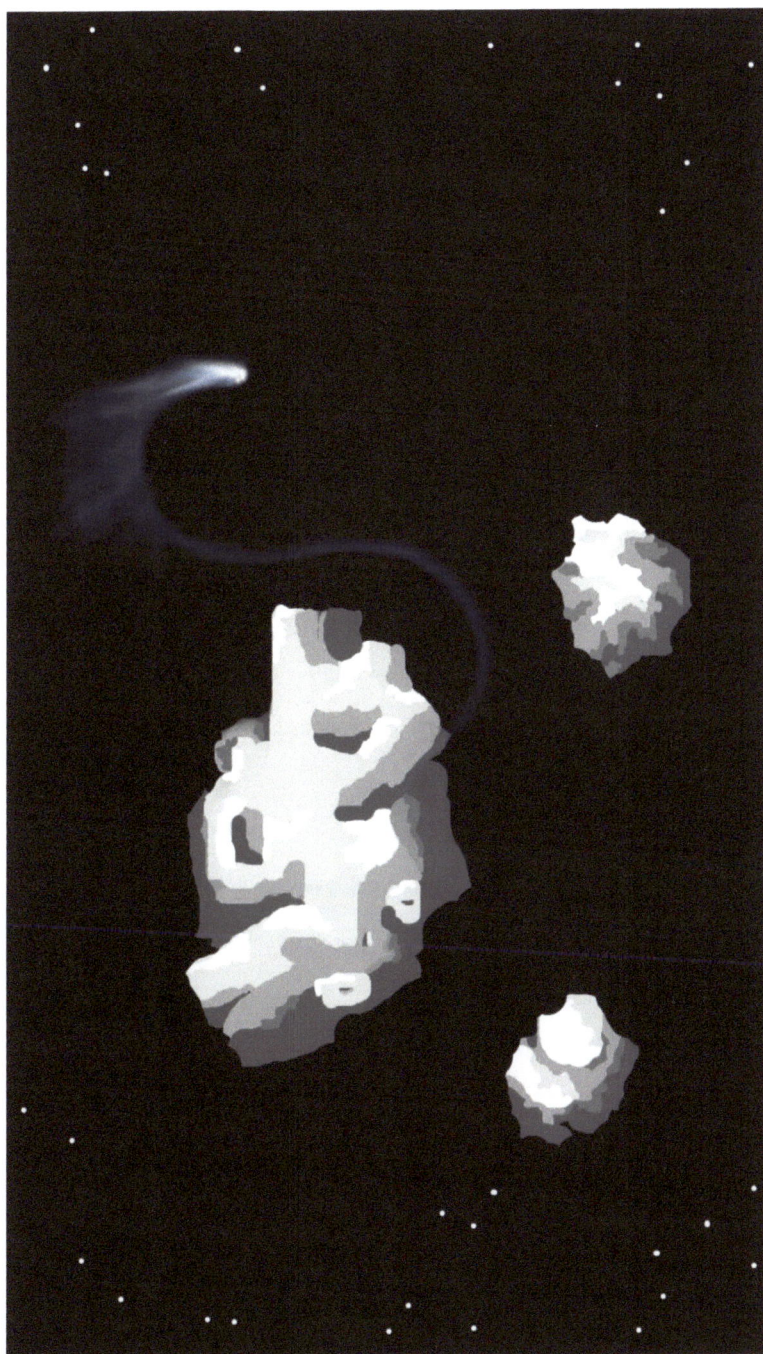

At last the comet came to a living planet
with no moon of its own.

"Oh planet, talk to me, be my friend,"
the comet called,
"I will tell you of my travels and you can
tell me of your dreams -- then perhaps
we can travel and dream together."

"Then love me," the planet answered.
"Here is your place, dance around me,
gaze into my blue-green beauty,
light my night skies and
never leave my side."

The comet tried.
She abandoned her journey, and
looped herself in a tight orbit
around the planet.
She dimmed her glow so its night skies
would not be too bright, and
she listened to the planet's stories.

But the orbit was too tight, and
the planet began to repeat itself, and
it did not want to hear of her travels or
to talk of far places.

"There can be nothing better than here,"
the planet said, "gaze at my glory
and forget the universe --
keep to your place as my moon."

Finally the comet knew she could not
stay -- she was a comet, not a moon.

She could not keep bending her nature
to an artificial orbit, and she could not
keep from longing for the distant stars.

So she unwrapped her orbit and left.

"Good riddance" called the planet
"you never were a good moon anyway."

And the comet traveled on,
toward the distant points of light.

After a time the comet reached one of
the points of light and it was huge!
It was a blazing ball of fire,
surrounded by a glorious radiance.
It was so big that she could orbit it
without contorting herself.

"Welcome," called the sun, "come closer
so I can admire you." And it drew her in.
Soon she was in a spinning dance,
whirling round and round in its pull.

"Look at my comet," the sun called out,
"How wonderful and powerful I must be,
to hold such a creature."

The comet began to feel weak from all the
spinning. She tried to slow down,
but the sun's grip was too strong.

He drew her tighter and tighter.
And she saw that she was shrinking,
loosing bits of herself,
for the sun was consuming her.

With a last desperate burst of energy,
the comet made her escape,
breaking off her tail like a lizard.

She left the sun roaring in rage
when it saw it had only a piece of her.

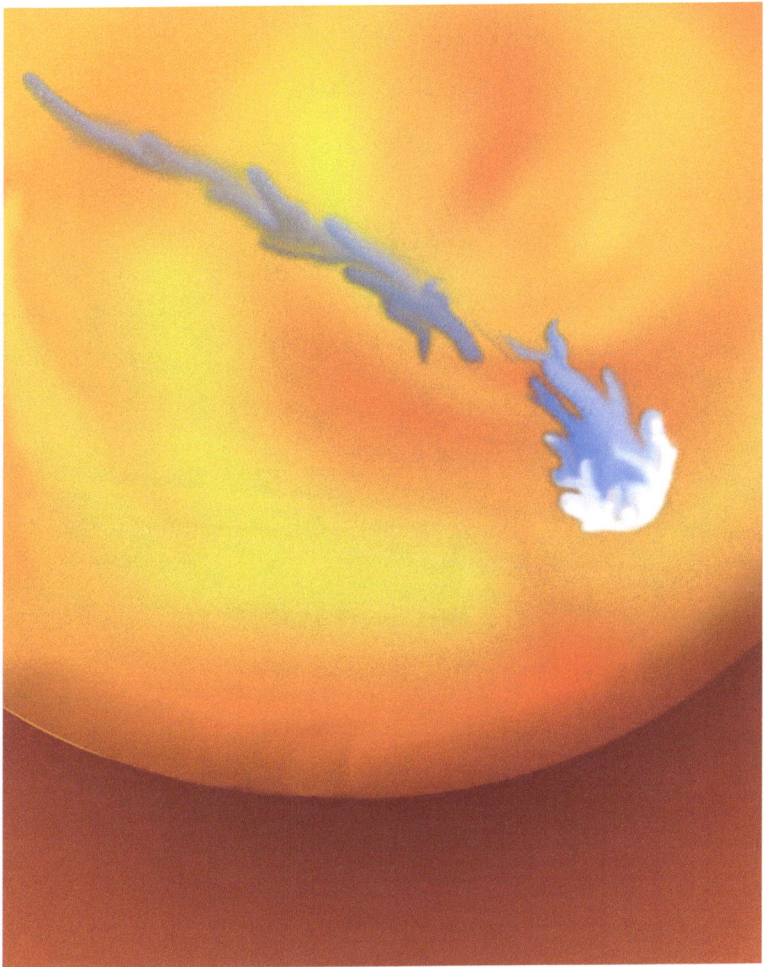

Deeply wounded,
the comet wandered aimlessly,
losing herself
in the night sky.

She sought the lonely,
frozen depths of space,
using the solitude
to rebuild herself.

Her tears froze
and became part of her being
as she slowly
regained her strength
and her sense of self.

After her long exile,
lonely beyond bearing,
the comet again sought
the distant points of light.

Traveling more cautiously now,
the comet approached a solar system.
It was filled with planets and moons, and
they all greeted her as she passed.

"Oh how beautiful you are," they called,
"stay awhile and tell us of your travels."

Hesitant at first, the comet drew closer.
Keeping her distance from the sun,
she danced among the planets,
decorating their night skies, and
telling them of her travels.

Slowly she grew confident enough to
approach the sun. Gradually she turned,
until her orbit was
close enough for sharing,
but far enough to avoid being consumed.

"Welcome," called the sun,
"How beautiful you are, and
how wonderful your tales of travel,
I've longed to travel like that myself."

So the comet told the sun of her travels
and listened to his dreams and to
his tales of the planets around him.
She basked in the warmth and acceptance
of the sun, his planets and their moons.

At long last all the stories had been told,
and the comet began to eye
the distant stars again.

"Come with me," she called to the sun,
"and we can travel together."

The sun sadly answered, "I cannot -- the
planets are dependent on me for the light
and warmth that sustain their life.
I cannot leave them."

The comet regarded the solar system
sadly. What the sun said was true --
he could not leave.

"But *you* must leave," said the sun, "it is
your nature to seek your dream -- go,
continue your journey,
but always know you are welcome
to return -- to come back and
tell us of your new travels and
recharge your glow from my warmth."

And so the comet traveled on . . .
alone, but no longer lonely.

THE END

ABOUT THE AUTHOR

BETSY A. RILEY was born in Kentucky in 1952. She spent her childhood and school years in Murray, Kentucky, graduating from Murray State University in 1973. She worked at Oak Ridge National Laboratory for over 37 years, before retiring to take a job with a federal agency. After three less than stellar marriages, she now lives happily in Damascus, Maryland, with her (fourth) husband Ken.